Sober Covenants

Sober Covenants

A Unique Perspective on
Big Book Promises
& Prayers

Andy C.
A Recovering Lawyer

Copyright © 2025 Andy C.

All rights reserved. This book or any portion thereof may not be reproduced or used in any manner whatsoever without the express written permission of the publisher except for the use of brief quotations in a book review.

ISBN: 9781990446214 (KDP Softcover)
ISBN: 9781990446221 (Ingram Hardcover)
ISBN: 9781990446238 (Ingram Softcover)
ISBN: 9781990446245 (Digital)

Contents

Preface		i
Introduction		1
Part 1:	The Step Nine Contract	3
Part 2:	The Lord's Prayer	63
Part 3:	Big Book Prayers	85

Preface

How this book came to be:
Every week the International Lawyers in AA (ILAA) meet online. We gather from around the world to share our experience, strength and hope in Recovery. There are downtown lawyers, shopping plaza lawyers, law students and judges, together with legal assistants and secretaries. There are multi-decade, kindling-dry old timers and young, still damp newcomers.

It is a great meeting.

Each week, there is a short peroration. These small essays are a selection from these closing comments; in legal jargon, these are "respectfully submitted."

The author hopes and prays that you enjoy them.

And speaking of the end, the author would remind everyone of the promise made by Bill H and others, "lawyers that stick around AA tend to do very well in the end."

By the way, you can join ILAA for free at ILAA.org.

Honoring Recovery:

In this book, the word Recovery is capitalized throughout. This choice reflects the profound and sacred role Recovery plays in the lives of those who walk its path. More than a process, Recovery is a shared identity, a source of hope and a spiritual journey. I chose to honor that by setting it apart typographically.

Caveat

These notes are personal thoughts and ruminations. They are not implicitly or expressly adopted, blessed or approved by Alcoholics Anonymous, International Lawyers in AA or any other person or body.

Some are my experiences, strengths and hopes, and have no more weight or meaning than any other share from a podium. Others are personal thoughts and views. Still others are observations from over 40 years of attending meetings and working in the Fellowship

Take what resonates and leave the rest.

Note on Authorship and Anonymity

In the Program of AA, we are anonymous, but privately, we can be open.

If you want to contact me, you can send me an email at the address below and I will strive to get back to you.

andyc@the4thdimension.ca

Proceeds

The writer and publisher hope to engender and enhance spiritual maintenance and will not profit monetarily from publishing this book. The books are priced at cost and any surplus cash will be dedicated to Recovery and Alcoholics Anonymous.

Twelve Steps of Alcoholics Anonymous

Step 1: We admitted we were powerless over alcohol—that our lives had become unmanageable.

Step 2: Came to believe that a Power greater than ourselves could restore us to sanity.

Step 3: Made a decision to turn our will and our lives over to the care of God as we understood Him.

Step 4: Made a searching and fearless moral inventory of ourselves.

Step 5: Admitted to God, to ourselves, and to another human being the exact nature of our wrongs.

Step 6: Were entirely ready to have God remove all these defects of character.

Step 7: Humbly asked Him to remove our shortcomings.

Step 8: Made a list of all persons we had harmed, and became willing to make amends to them all.

Step 9: Made direct amends to such people wherever possible, except when to do so would injure them or others.

Step 10: Continued to take personal inventory and when we were wrong promptly admitted it.

Step 11: Sought through prayer and meditation to improve our conscious contact with God, as we understood Him, praying only for knowledge of His will for us and the power to carry that out.

Step 12: Having had a spiritual awakening as the result of these Steps, we tried to carry this message to alcoholics, and to practice these principles in all our affairs.

Introduction

At ILAA meetings, we close each meeting with a reading of the Step Nine Promises in the Big Book and the Lord's Prayer.

When I assumed the 'closing duties' for our weekly online meetings, I decided to change it up a bit.

I submitted to the group that the Step Nine Promises could be seen as a contract. I could review it clause by clause, applying legal tools of deconstruction and analysis to this Step Nine Contract. Each week I shared some interpretive thoughts on a clause of that contract.

This approach was met with approbation.

As mentioned, the usual closing procedure included a recital of the Lord's Prayer.

It seemed natural to offer a clause-by-clause commentary on the Lord's Prayer. So after I reviewed the Step Nine Contract clauses, I began a weekly clause-by-clause review, assisted by Emmet Fox's excellent essay in Sermon on the Mount. Each week I dwelt on one clause from that great prayer.

Again, this approach was well received.

I was on a roll, so with the approval of the Group, I turned next to the Big Book. I went through some of the more salient prayers; deconstructing and analyzing each one as I had done with the clause-by-clause review of the Step Nine Contract and Lord's Prayer.

These are the thoughts presented each week to the International Lawyers in AA Zoom meeting: the Step Nine Contract, the Lord's Prayer and selected Big Book prayers. 🖋

PART ONE

Step Nine Promises

Introduction

As lawyers, we understand contracts; we draft them and interpret them.

Contracts are promises; promises are contracts. I submit the promises listed in Step Nine of our program can be read and interpreted as a contract; therefore, a legalistic deconstruction is useful.

Conducting a clause-by-clause analysis, we can see truths and meanings, often overlooked in a reading of the Step Nine promises at the end of an AA meeting. This is a deeper legalistic dive into a very important contract. 🔖

Step Nine Promises

Quoting from The Big Book of Alcoholics Anonymous:

> If we are painstaking about this phase of our development, we will be amazed before we are halfway through. We are going to know a new freedom and a new happiness. We will not regret the past nor wish to shut the door on it. We will comprehend the word serenity and we will know peace. No matter how far down the scale we have gone, we will see how our experience can benefit others. That feeling of uselessness and self-pity will disappear. We will lose interest in selfish things and gain interest in our fellows. Self-seeking will slip away. Our whole attitude and outlook upon life will change. Fear of people and of economic insecurity will leave us. We will intuitively know how to handle situations which used to baffle us. We will suddenly realize that God is doing

for us what we could not do for ourselves. Are these extravagant promises? We think not. They are being fulfilled among us—sometimes quickly, sometimes slowly. They will always materialize if we work for them." ✏

Consideration, Part #1 - Standard of Performance

Contracts are often "if…then" propositions. If you do this, you will get that.

If an action or effort is stipulated as consideration in a service contract, and the effort is made or action is taken, *then* the contract will be honored. And many service contracts stipulate a standard of performance for the delivery of the effort or action to be taken.

The Step Nine Contract is not a contract for property or goods, it is a service contract. To enforce the terms of the contract and obtain the benefits thereof, we must perform specific actions and meet a stipulated performance standard.

I want to first look at the stipulated standard of performance that must be met.

Stipulating a service or effort to be performed to a defined standard as consideration in a contract is not unusual.

For example, a service contract might read, "if the Party of the First Part uses his/her reasonable commercial efforts to…, then the Party of the Second Part will honor its obligations under the contract." The Party of the Second Part honors his obligations in return for the effort of the Party of the First Part, and that effort must meet a certain standard. The standard of effort is defined by a phrase that can be looked up in a legal dictionary: "reasonable commercial effort."

The opening clause of our Step Nine Contract sets a performance standard, which is: "painstaking."

This is a word that is easily understood. A plain reading of the word suggests that taking pains to achieve something is to be painstaking. The Oxford Dictionary defines painstaking as "extremely careful and correct, involving a lot of effort." Synonyms listed in that dictionary include "careful, meticulous and thorough."

If the AA member is painstaking, that is, if the AA is "extremely careful, correct, and works hard," then certain contracted consequences will follow.

And God, as I have understood Him, determines whether I have made the effort to the required standard.

This is fortunate. The alternative to an assessment by God might be an assessment by a sponsor, and sponsors rarely give reasonable judgments.

In the following note, I turn to the effort which is to be painstaking. 🖋

Consideration, Part #2 - What is to be done

As we saw in the last note, the Step Nine Contract is a service contract which stipulates a standard of performance, which is "painstaking." To be painstaking, we must be thorough and take great care.

But what is the object of our thoroughness and care? What is the service to be performed or effort to be made, the consideration which must be provided to enforce the contract?

The service consideration of this contract is taking the Steps and applying the principles thoroughly enough to allow us to say that at "this phase of our development," we call for the rewards promised in the contract. The relevant clause reads, "If we are painstaking about this phase of our development," then the Step Nine covenants will come true.

But in a contract, consideration must be defined with some precision, enough that a third party could agree that it was done. So we are entitled to ask, what exactly is "this phase of our development"? How many of the Steps and principles must we complete, and what exactly does this phrase mean?

The contract appears to relate to the Step Nine promises, so "this phase of our development" could be a reference to making amends, so before we are halfway through Step Nine, the promises will come true? Or "this phase of our development" could mean the whole amends process, so the promises will come true before we are halfway through Steps Eight and Nine? Or might "this phase of our development" be a reference to all the work done up to and including Step Nine amends?

I have heard this question debated vigorously by AA Big Book fundamentalists. Such conversations always remind me of Dan M, a lawyer in AA, and his theory of how AA works and why we have The Big Book.

Quoting Dan, "Bill and Bob met and talked; they stayed sober by talking and talking and talking over countless cups of coffee. They brought others into the conversations, and they all talked and talked.

One day, they all ran out of things to talk about; the silence was deafening; our Founders grew afraid.

"They realized that as long as two or more alcoholics talked to each other, they stayed sober. But how could this work if they ran out of things to talk about? Future AAs needed an everlasting source of things to talk about.

"They hit on the idea of a textbook for the program. They would use different words in the textbook for the same things, like defects and shortcomings. They would introduce minor points of potential confusion, like referring to both moral and personal inventories. And they would have minor contradictions and ambiguities, not enough to affect the integrity of the process, but enough to cause conversations, all designed to keep AAs talking.

"Now," the Founders said, "with this Big Book, future alcoholics will always have something to talk about!"

I think Bill's use of "this phase of development" is an example of this theory of The Big Book. It is a slightly ambiguous clause in an otherwise clear language contract. A phrase that we could argue over and discuss for days and be no further ahead or behind. But talking to each other, we will stay sober.

Humor aside, as lawyers, we cannot duck the issue when faced with contracts which are ambiguous or allow for different interpretations. We must construe the words to give practical effect to the Parties' apparent intent.

I submit the following as a practical construction of the phrase, which will fulfill the intent of the Parties: "If I am painstaking about our processes—our Twelve Steps—then the promises in the contract will be enforceable."

Under this construction, the word *halfway* might be a red herring. The draftsman of the Contract could have said "immediately" instead of "halfway through," and it would not have changed the effect. After all, what is halfway through our Program, which is a lifetime program? It is only complete when, as a friend of mine says, "They throw a shovel of dirt on my face."

Or maybe the promises come true halfway through each iteration of the Steps. Perhaps the promises become truer every time we do the Twelve Steps. This construction embraces all the Steps, which cannot be bad. For starters, it would include Steps Ten, Eleven, and Twelve.

Either way, the effort to be made in consideration of the promises is the painstaking application of our Twelve Step processes in our lives, the Program, sponsorship and service. The whole package.

I submit this interpretation because, in my experience, if I am painstaking about applying all the principles of the Program, the promised benefits have come in ever larger amounts with each application. ✒

The First Promise

Now we turn our attention to the next phrase in the contract, which is the first consequence of being painstaking; we will be surprised and astonished. To quote from the contract, "we will be amazed."

We who have worked with newcomers or watched people change as they attend meetings know this to be true.

I remember a fellow in our home group. He was cantankerous and difficult. Every week, he shared about his difficult wife and what a burden he carried.

One week, his sponsor told him, "You are going to look after the tea and coffee for the meetings." The sponsee argued but ultimately agreed.

He arrived early and prepared the tea and coffee. And he did this every week.

Our meeting was a topic and discussion format, and the group was small. Everyone had a chance to share.

Over the following weeks, his shares changed. He stopped complaining about his home life and spoke about his wife in a different and positive tone.

Many meetings later, he opened up about the changes he experienced in making coffee for the meetings, how the simple act of serving others was a breakthrough experience.

He recalled, "I was making coffee for the second week, and I thought, this is what my wife does for me every day; I should be grateful."

He continued, "That broke the dam; I changed my attitudes and perceptions. It took time, but that was where it started."

I was amazed. Almost as surprised as he was. He was halfway through something, and the change was amazing.

In the rooms of AA, we see many such changes. We are constantly amazed, astonished, and surprised.

But there is another side to this promise. We also know the pain of watching someone who comes to the Program and does not put any effort into the Steps. They never get halfway to anywhere; therefore, the promises are not enforceable.

In these cases, we are neither amazed nor surprised.

The outcomes are sad and certain. We watch as they spiral back to drinking. We almost cry when, predictably, they don't show up for meetings, screen their phone calls and don't return emails.

We are relieved and happy if, having found a new bottom, they return. But they do not always make it back.

Surprise and astonishment are two excellent barometers of "painstakingness." Rarely have we seen a person fail to amaze and surprise if they are painstaking, and rarely have we seen a person succeed if they are not. 🖋

Freedom and Happiness

We have looked at the performance standard of the contract, "painstaking," the service or effort, "this phase of our development," and the first promissory clause of the contract: "we will be amazed."

The next clauses are subordinate to, but do not limit, the promise of the first clause. They list detailed examples of why "we will be amazed."

The first example is uncomplicated, but complex; "we will be amazed" because "we are going to know a new freedom and happiness."

This one sentence has five separate elements: *We are / going to know / a new / freedom and / happiness.*

1. We are
We, that is us. Conjoining the words *we* and *are* creates a special grammatical case which is highly predictive with a strong sense of immediacy; this sets the tone of the promise. It is going to be immediate and highly likely to occur.

2. going to know

This little phrase packs an interpretive wallop.

The preposition *to* is shared with the two verbs *going* and *know*, creating two sub-phrases, *going to* and *to know*. I will consider both phrases in turn.

Grammatically, the phrase *going to* indicates future tense, the promise of a future condition, event, or state.

And the phrase *to know* is the infinitive case which imparts a sense of infinite, a sense of something that is continuous and expanding.

Knowledge is not attitudes, feelings, or emotions. These are transient. Knowledge is permanent. It becomes part of our being; it is ontological. Once we know something, it is part of us.

Bringing it all together: *with a high degree of certainty and almost immediately, we will gain knowledge which may expand infinitely and will change our being.*

3. a new

An article and adjective. The dictionary meaning of the adjective *new* is "recent, beginning, different from some category that had existed before." Echoes of being surprised and amazed are associated with this word; it echoes the promise of astonishment in a grounded fashion. It applies to the next two words.

4. freedom and

Freedom means release from a prior state. For an alcoholic, it means freedom from the desire to drink and, still later, with subsequent spiritual awakenings, comes to mean freedom and release from the bondage of self. These are both states of being that are enjoyed and experienced, and both are new to a recovering alcoholic.

The conjunctive *and* is self-explanatory, both freedom and the next word, *happiness,* are conjoined.

5. happiness

Happiness means a state of well-being and satisfaction. Not traipsing through the tulips, but something heftier and more significant; it means well-being and satisfaction, not giggles and popcorn.

Like freedom, for an alcoholic, this is new.

In conclusion, this first subordinate clause is both uncomplicated and complex. ❧

The Power of the Past

If I meet the performance standard of working on the Program in a painstaking manner, I can expect the contracted deliverables.

As a side note, if I am not experiencing the deliverables, perhaps I am not painstaking in working on my program; the contract is not enforceable because of a failure of consideration.

But let's return to the primary focus, the deliverables in the Step Nine Contract. The first deliverable is amazing change, and thereafter, the Contract lists some examples of the amazing change.

The first example, which I considered in the preceding note, was "We are going to know a new freedom and happiness."

The second, the subject of this note, is "We will not regret the past nor wish to shut the door on it."

What is *regret*? Turning to my dictionary, I find that it can be used as a verb or a noun. As a noun, it is an emotional state that includes sadness, repentance, or disappointment over the past, either about what

Step Nine Promises 23

has happened or opportunities missed. As a verb, it means to experience that emotional state.

For alcoholics, for whom half-measures are never enough, sadness, regret and disappointment are amplified to shame, fear, and remorse.

When this promise is fulfilled, when we remember the past, we will no longer experience these feelings. The past will lose its grip on us. As a result, I will not wish to shut the door on my past. I can recall the past without fear, I can play the movie and not have the feelings.

Let me share a personal experience.

Years ago, I was the center of a national Canadian newspaper, television, and social media storm.

The storm, after several weeks, died down. For a long time, I suppressed all memory of the event and the media storm. I stuffed it deep and shut the door on it, thinking I was putting it behind me.

But the door would not stay shut. Occasionally, it blew open, like a door catching a gust of wind, blowing open and slamming against the wall.

I had not thought about that episode for some time. Assuming the whole episode was long past, an AA friend joked about the event and the media storm. It was completely innocent and should have been harmless. But it was not; it was an emotional arrow into my heart. The gust of wind caught the door, and it was blown open and slammed against the wall.

In an instant, I replayed the whole movie of that dark time and relived all the feelings. The pressure from the stuffed feelings had been silently building and when released, those feelings surged up with an intensity I can still recall to this day. The promise of the past losing its grip was not fulfilled. At once, shame, anger, disappointment and fear returned; I had to struggle to shut the door.

But partway through the struggle, I realized this promise was not being fulfilled; I thought I had been painstaking, but if I had met the standard of performance, the contract would be honored. I had not met the standard. I started to work on it.

I painstakingly applied the principles of the Program to this long-past event and the associated media storm. Years later, after inventories, conversations with God and my spiritual coach, amends, prayer and Step work, someone else made a joke about the event. I was untouched. I could recall it and play the movie without the feelings. Instead of regret, I felt a sense of impartial neutrality and serenity.

I was amazed. I had not believed such a condition would come to pass.

For that event, the promise is now true, I do not feel regret, and I have no wish to shut the door on it. The whole incident has lost its grip on my soul. All because I paid the consideration for the promise. ✒

Serenity and Peace

The next example of amazing change that is listed is "We will comprehend the word serenity and we will know peace."

This clause consists of two phrases joined by a conjunctive *and*.

Both phrases, *we will comprehend the word serenity* and *we will know peace,* contain the word *will*, a modal verb, with a particular grammatical meaning: the affirmation of necessity, pointing to an inevitable eventuality, fact or certainty. The modal property implies that if the required actions are performed to the standard of performance, the promises in these phrases are inevitable and certain.

The promises are contained in the four operative words of the two phrases, two verbs: *comprehend* and *know*. The verbs have two objects: the words *serenity* and *peace*.

Serenity and *peace* are nearly synonymous. Both are states of being a person can occupy or possess.

Serenity is a state of being calm, peaceful and untroubled. Peace is tranquility, mental calm and serenity. Both words are nouns with an active sense; they are experienced and lived, not static and observed. The variations in the shades of meaning between the two words, serenity and peace, are distinctions with no differences.

If *peace* and *serenity* are nearly synonymous, why use two phrases? Why the redundancy? I submit that the purpose of the redundancy lies in the two verbs: *comprehend* and *know*. We will comprehend the word *serenity* and *know* peace. And we need both.

Comprehend versus Know: To *comprehend* is to grasp mentally or understand, in this case, the meaning of a word. To mentally grasp and understand *serenity* is to skim its surface. It is nice to have, but not life-altering. To comprehend is not to possess.

But the second verb is something else; to *know* something is to experience it. To *know* something is more personal and profound than to *comprehend* something. To know something is to incorporate it into our being. It is ontological.

We need both; comprehension improves knowledge. To know something without comprehension is good, but it is difficult to pass on to anyone else, and perhaps difficult to maintain. Comprehension perfects and deepens knowledge.

With the near synonymity of *serenity* and *peace*, we can conflate and apply *comprehension* and *knowledge* to both *serenity* and *peace*. With the modal verb *will*, we are promised comprehension and knowledge of serenity and peace with certainty.

I love the Step Nine Contract, particularly this powerful covenant. 🖋

Our Worst Becomes Our Best

We have completed the examples of amazing changes. The next Article in the Step Nine Contract is a promise: "No matter how far down the scale we have gone, we will see how our experience can benefit others."

Earlier, I shared the story of my national media shaming. That experience brought me far down the scale. At its nadir, I was the target of vicious gossip. I saw my name on the little screens in downtown elevators. I was disinvited to chair a major fundraiser for a treatment center which I had founded, and I was disinvited to supper parties, I was a social pariah.

But, as described in the last note, after painstakingly applying the principles of the Program, I no longer regretted that part of my past and did not wish to shut the door on it.

But seeing how that experience could benefit anyone, that's another story, and here it is.

Years later, a politician I knew created his own media storm. He was shamed and humiliated in the press. I could easily identify with his situation. The stories were still making the front pages. He was avoiding public activities like grocery shopping.

Though I did not know him well, I could see his plight and identify with his likely feelings of shame and fear. I decided to call him to let him know that someone cared about him, and remind him that this too shall pass.

He was avoiding talking to angry callers by directing all his calls to voicemail.

I left a message, "Hi, don't erase this message, this is a friendly call. I have been where you are. You are not getting many friendly calls today, but this is one. Give me a call if you want friendly chat."

He called back and we met for coffee.

To my knowledge, he was not an alcoholic, just a fellow person who was publicly humiliated. I had no purpose other than to show him that there was life after a shaming in the media and press.

We met and I shared the story of my media humiliation and how it had affected my family and me. He nodded as I told of my fear, anger, and shame. As with me, his family was included in the public humiliation. We had much in common.

We got to joking about politics and life as a politician. He talked about constituent calls, voters who were never at fault and demanded the passage of laws to solve their problems. He shared how he tried to put them off as gently as possible. He had to listen to them, and they talked forever.

I laughed and then told him I was involved in AA, and that we had sponsees in AA. I said, "They are like constituents; they have issues, but it is never their fault. Someone should immediately pass a law. And they too can talk forever!

"But we AA sponsors have an *aha* button. A button that says 'aha' when you press it. Politicians need aha buttons on their desks."

He laughed.

It was a great conversation; I thought it had lifted his spirits. But there was more, much more. After we laughed, he became silent and serious, "You said you were involved in AA, I did not know this side of you. I am more grateful for this time than ever... I think I have a drinking problem."

He was surprised to find I was in AA and I was surprised by his admission. Regardless, we got to work. He is now a successful and serving member of AA. He sponsors, does Twelve Step work and has started meetings.

I could not have called my new AA friend if I had not created a media storm, then painstakingly worked the program to recover. But I did and, not regretting the past nor wishing to shut the door on it, I discovered that God apparently had a use for it. It created a 12-Step call.

This is a powerful deliverable in the Step Nine Contract. One that many lawyers in AA have experienced. ✣

The Engine of Growth

The next clause in our analysis is a long promise with several moving parts; it reads as follows: "That feeling of uselessness and self-pity will disappear. We will lose interest in selfish things and gain interest in our fellows. Self-seeking will slip away."

Before I start this note, let me digress.

I am a solicitor; I draft contracts and documents. Over the years, litigators have torn my contracts apart, then assert to their clients, judges and anyone else who will listen, "The draftsman of the contract, Andy, failed to state the intent of the parties clearly."

Then these same lawyers suggest a different construction that more clearly reflects the intent of the draftsman.

I never liked this, but learned that sometimes they were correct. Their reconstruction was better; the meaning was unchanged, and with the revisions, it was more clearly expressed.

I submit that we can reconstruct the phrases contained in these three sentences, not to change the meaning, but to better show how the elements of the sentences work together.

Here is my suggested construction of this clause: There is one operative phrase, which is the consideration for the enforceability of four promises in the remaining phrases. The operative phrase, the axis around which the four promises revolve, states that we will "gain interest in our fellows."

The four promises which will come true as a direct result of our gaining interest in our fellows:

- That feeling of uselessness will disappear,
- That feeling of self-pity will disappear,
- We lose interest in selfish things, and
- Self-seeking will slip away.

The best way to gain interest in our fellows is to be painstaking about applying the Program and working the Steps in all our affairs, the consideration and standard of performance for the Step Nine Contract.

Working the Program takes our attention away from ourselves and our problems and turns us to think about others. We strive to help suffering alcoholics. As a consequence, these four promises come true.

That, I submit, is a better construction of these clauses.

I imagine a metaphorical train sitting at an imaginary station.

The locomotive at the front of the train is named "Gaining Interest in Our Fellows." *Fellows* includes our family, fellow workers, partners, and our clients. Thinking about others and becoming interested in them, we build up steam in the boiler, and the locomotive starts to move down the tracks.

Behind the locomotive are three cars and a caboose. The cars carry the three feelings: uselessness, self-pity and self-seeking, and in the caboose are selfish things. The engine pulls away and the whole train starts to move down the track.

Chugga chugga choo choo, the program train pulls out of the station, with all four promises in tow.

Just gain interest in our fellows and the rest will follow.

Woooo Wooo! 🚂

Four Big Ones

As we continue our analysis of the Step Nine Contract, we turn to the following sentences, which I group together as the Clause Seven of the contract:

1. "Our whole attitude and outlook upon life will change.

2. "Fear of people and of economic insecurity will leave us.

3. "We will intuitively know how to handle situations which used to baffle us.

4. "We will suddenly realize that God is doing for us what we could not do for ourselves."

I have grouped these sentences together in one clause, Clause Seven of the Step Nine Contract. But how are we to construe this Clause? The sentences seem simple. But there may be more here than first meets the eye.

I submit to you two possible constructions of Clause Seven.

A possible first interpretation: The first sentence or subclause, "Our whole attitude and outlook on life will change," is a broad principal promise of attitudinal and outlook change. This central promise is followed by three sentences which are examples of the changes we can expect from this primary change: removal of fear, provision of intuitive solutions and God doing things for us we could not do ourselves.

In a second alternate interpretation, there are four separate promises, one for each sentence, each standing alone.

Before starting this analysis we should, at least briefly, consider whether there is a practical difference between the two interpretations and, if so, whether the difference means anything.

I submit that there is a practical difference, and the difference is not meaningless.

If the first sentence is a primary promise of change in outlook and attitude, followed by three examples of the change, then there is an implied limit to the changes we can expect. If the following three promises are constituents of the central promise, the rule of *ejusdem generis* may apply. This rule suggests that the changes in attitude and outlook in the principal clause should be construed as being limited to the class or kind of the subsequent listed series.

Applying this canon, the character of the promised change of "our whole attitude and outlook" would be limited to the class and kind of the subclauses listed below the first sentence.

On the other hand, if there are four separate promises, the rule of *ejusdem generis* does not apply. Therefore, the first clause, a warranty, "our whole attitude and outlook on life will change," is followed by three promises. Each of these promises can be read without any limit implied by *ejusdem generis*.

Which interpretation prevails?

First, I direct your attention to Bill's grammar in the three promises. He ends each statement with a period rather than a comma or semicolon. While the presence of a period versus a comma is not conclusive, separate sentences are suggestive of four distinct promises.

However, another more salient point must be noted. The first sentence promises change, an open-ended covenant, with no guidance as to the change which will take place. To merely promise change is not complete. The nature of the change might be implied to be good, but as an alcoholic I know not all change is good change. When I drank, I changed, but in a bad way. We would have to "read in" all manner of positive adverbs to qualify the nature of the change to make constructive and positive sense of this sentence. Applying Occam's Razor to this problem, the simpler version is better, making this the less desirable interpretation.

The better reading would therefore appear to be the first interpretation: a general promise of change followed by three examples of the change, examples which are positive and constructive, good change.

The open-ended sense of the first promise trumps the grammatical suggestion of separate thoughts separated by periods. The *ejusdem generis* canon of construction, would apply.

Therefore, our whole attitude and outlook will change, illustrated by three examples: removal of fear, intuitive knowledge and God's help. In the next notes, I continue this meditation, exploring the result of applying the legal canon, *ejusdem generis,* in this clause of the Step Nine Contract. ✒

Change

I have argued Clause Seven is properly construed as a principal promise of change, followed by a listed series of examples of change. In the following notes, I will consider the principal clause and the three illustrative sub-clauses.

The principal promise is:

"Our whole attitude and outlook upon life will change."

And the illustrative subclauses are:

"Fear of people and of economic insecurity will leave us.

"We will intuitively know how to handle situations which used to baffle us.

"We will suddenly realize that God is doing for us what we could not do for ourselves."

In this note, I will dwell on the principal clause, "Our whole attitude and outlook upon life will change."

Structurally, the word "whole" modifies "attitude." Half measures are not contemplated in this promise. It is our whole attitude, not a part. Turning to Webster's Dictionary, an attitude is a settled or usual way of thinking about something, typically reflected in our behavior. And this whole set will change. And it does not promise to change our circumstances or our conditions. The promise is limited to our attitude, it is an inside job.

Which brings the discussion to the word *outlook*. Outlook could refer to a vantage point from which we view, or the view itself. The phrase *upon life* suggests that it is the vantage point and not the view. We cannot look *upon* a view of life, but we can look upon our life.

Outlooks or vantage points are important. You will only see trees if you are on the ground in a forest. It is likely dark and fearful. If your vantage point is elevated to a mountain top, you see the earth's contours and the bright blue sky. You can admire the wonders of the world.

But this refers to "our outlook upon life." This vantage point is not physical; it is internal, spiritual, or mental. It is our cognitive mapping of the world. We could have a vantage point or outlook standing in the forest of life with a view of the trees and little sunlight. Or we could have an elevated mountain top vantage point, a Higher Power vantage point.

Our vantage point determines our outlook upon life and our mapping of the world, and changing it makes a difference.

I want to touch briefly on the word *whole*, and whether it touches the question of our outlook or vantage point of our life. The word *whole* does not necessarily modify *outlook*. As we have determined, *outlook* in this context is a vantage point; one stands on an outlook and surveys the world. If the adjective *whole* modifies a subject, the subject must be scalable; there must be partials and degrees, a less than whole and a whole. A vantage point, unlike an attitude, does not have partials or degrees; it is a "fixed point," a position from which we view.

But the nature of the change is not at this point clear. All we are promised is a whole change in attitude and change in our outlook upon life. We assume and hope the changes will be good, but to see the nature of the change we must continue to read the Contract. We find the nature of the changes in the class and kind of the listed series of changes following this principal promise of change. ✒

First- and Second-Order Effects

I have argued Clause Seven is properly construed as a general promise, "Our whole attitude and outlook upon life will change," followed by three examples:

"Fear of people and of economic insecurity will leave us.

"We will intuitively know how to handle situations which used to baffle us.

"We will suddenly realize that God is doing for us what we could not do for ourselves."

Having considered the principal promise of change, I now turn to the first subclause, the first example of change, "Fear of people and of economic insecurity will leave us."

This sentence promises two categories of fear will depart. With respect to people, the promise focuses on a first-order effect, fear of people. With respect to our economic life, the promise focuses on a second order, the fear of insecurity arising from our economic situation.

The first promise is, "fear of people will be removed." The removal of fear of people is a first order effect. We will fear no man, woman, or thing. We will not cross the street to avoid people. We will not screen our calls. We will not fear anyone.

But this promise does not include relief from the second-order effects of people—joys and difficulties in relationships. The second order relationship effects associated with people can include hurt, abandonment, or harm; we are not promised relief or protection from these. We will have all the problems (and joys) of relationships with people. But we will not fear the people, which enhances the chances of a good relationship outcome.

The second promise, "fear of economic insecurity will leave us," does not deal with the first order problem of economic insecurity. It deals only with the second order effect: fear arising from economic insecurity. The first-order problem, economic insecurity, may still be with us. But we are promised relief with respect to the second-order effect of economic security: fear arising therefrom.

This contract was written in the depths of the depression in the United States of America. Bill would have preferred that God deal with the first order problem and remove his economic insecurity. But that is not the promise. The promise deals with fear of economic insecurity, the second-order effect. We may still be economically insecure, but we will not fear it. And as with fear of people, being unafraid of economic insecurity will often increase the chances of a good economic outcome.

Two promises, both dealing with fear; one dealing with a first-order effect and the other with a second-order effect.

As we consider this promise, there is more to be seen, a fascinating process point; these fears "leave us." We don't excise them, fight them, or force them out. They just leave us. Much as we lost the desire to drink, these fears leave.

So, if we meet the standards of performance in our effort in the Program and are painstaking in applying this Program in our lives, our attitude and outlook will change, fear of people will leave us, and, in regard to our economic needs, fear of insecurity will leave us. ✒

Intuition, Practice Perfects

The second example of the promised change, "We will intuitively know how to handle situations which used to baffle us."

Life is baffling, but if we are painstaking about using the Program in all our affairs, which is stipulated as the consideration for the promises, this will come true: We will intuitively know how to handle life and all it throws at us.

In our painstaking application of the principles of the Program, we practice Steps Three and Eleven; we seek knowledge of God's will.

We seek, but how do we hear or see the answer? How is God's will communicated to us? Does God's finger write on the wall? Do we have a manual or script to follow? How do we discern God's will for us? In this subclause, Bill provides an answer to this question—intuition.

Intuition is a felt sense rather than conscious reasoning. Bill refers to intuition frequently. Here and elsewhere, he writes about a growing sense of confidence in our intuition as we practice the Program.

Our Founders were members of the Oxford Group; as Oxforders, they practiced Guidance. Sitting quietly in prayer with pen and paper, they asked God questions about what to do and when to do it, then waited for knowledge of God's will to emerge, writing down intuitive thoughts that came to mind.

Some who don't frame God in the phrase "Higher Power" may query this promise of divine intuition. However, I submit, it still applies. The preparation for the intuition is to become quiet, soberly meditate on the good, then listen with an open heart. If all I hear in reply is an intuition from my subconscious, so be it. It is an intuition developed while my heart and mind were calm and oriented to the best. How bad could that be?

Either way, from God or our better selves, we find that we intuit more and more. Bill refers to "a growing sense of confidence in our intuition." We start with intuitions on small things and, with practice, learn to rely on them for larger and more important issues. We start, then get better; we improve with practice.

But even intuitions from God should be checked. Members of the Oxford Group learned that their first intuition, especially when they were beginning their practice of Guidance, might not be a good idea; it might be their ego imitating an intuition from God. They knew it took time and practice to recognize the true from the false ideas. They learned to "check their Guidance" with a close, trusted advisor.

And if we are filling our intuitions with our own ego thoughts, the Guidance can be bad or silly, even with a good orientation. If you get an intuition to take your rent money and bet on a winning horse, you might check first with an AA friend. If you intuit that you are now cured and can safely drink again, check first with your sponsor.

Whatever the source of my intuition—divinity or my subconscious—it is a good rule to "check my Guidance" before executing.

If we are painstaking about our Program, we will get in touch with our intuitions. And as we practice our Program, we will become more comfortable with our intuitions.

As promised, we will intuitively know how to handle situations that used to baffle us. 🌠

An Inside Job

The third subclause of Clause Seven is the third example of change: "We will suddenly realize God is doing for us what we could not do for ourselves."

A great promise, but again, how is it delivered; how and when will we see it?

To answer this, I remind you of the canon of construction, *ejusdem generis*; anything listed as part of a series will be construed to be consistent with the same class or kind of the other elements in the series. The preceding promises are interior promises; that is, their class and kind.

Let me elaborate. The class or kind of the preceding examples are attitudes and outlooks, fears and intuitions. These are part of the "inside job." God does not promise to shape the world to make us feel better. He removes our fear, an interior phenomenon. He does not change the baffling situations; He gives us intuitions on how to deal with them, an interior phenomenon. The examples of change in the preceding series share a common characteristic:

He works on our insides. On our own, we could not remove the fears of economic insecurity or people; we could only react to these fears with anger or shame. On our own, we did not handle situations that baffled us; we often ran away or lashed out. But God worked on our insides and gave us interior power.

Applying the rule of *ejusdem generis* and construing the third promise, God will work on our interiors, and "do for us what we could not do for ourselves."

I submit therefore, that in this third example of change, God does not promise to fix life for us; instead, we will be fixed to meet life as it is.

Working with our insides, God will "do for us what we could not do for ourselves."

Don't look for changes in your circumstances or conditions, look for changes in your attitudes, outlook and thoughts. These are the interior things that God, or the universal power, can and will work with. The things that we could not change ourselves. ✿

Introduction to the End

We are near the end of the contract with two remaining sentences: "Are these extravagant promises? We think not."

The last clause begins with an interrogatory phrase, *Are the promises made herein extravagant?* And rhetorically responds, *No!*

We must give meaning to all the words and clauses in a contract. What did Bill mean when he wrote this? The first thought that occurred to me was that the draftsman is worried that the reader of the contract will doubt the *bona fides* of the promises.

These promises are extraordinary and very difficult to achieve. Therefore, he poses the question for us, *Are these extravagant?*

Bill, who trained briefly as a lawyer, could have written a clause like, "We warrant that these are reasonable promises and can be achieved," or "The promises made herein are deliverable and reasonable within the boundaries of the performance of typical alcoholics."

Instead, he uses a theatrical call-and-answer flourish, a psychological trick to cause a pause, and force us to consider the question. Then, with a Yoda-like twist of phrase, he answers his own question with the phrase often repeated out loud at meetings, "We think not."

All in all, it is an exciting and clever introduction to the final clause, which affirms the sanctity of the Ninth Step Contract. 🖋

Promises Fulfilled

After the call and answer, "Are these extravagant promises? We think not." Bill gives a warranty to all the Promises. He gives the warranty as a statement of fact.

"They are being fulfilled among us."

Deconstructing this sentence, "they" refers to the promises in the Step Nine Contract.

Are and *being* are both forms of the verb *to be*. The meaning of the verb *to be* is to occur or take place. *Are* is the third-person plural of the verb *to be* and, in this sentence, is an auxiliary verb creating a sense of "continuousness."

And *being* is the present participle—not the past participle—of the verb *to be*. This promise will take place in the present, not the future, and neither is it a past phenomenon which is spent.

In summary, "are being" means the subject, the promises, are occurring or taking place at this time, and continuously.

"Fulfilled" means coming true, maturing into reality. The promises are maturing, becoming real.

And all of this is a statement of fact, not theory. Facts which are being established among us, the members of the Fellowship. All AAs who are meeting the standard of performance are experiencing all the promises. This language inheres two elements: an implied conditional promise and a warranty; to wit, if you are like us, it will work for you.

So far, this is straightforward. But I submit a further observation for your consideration: that in this warranty, there is a subliminal lesson about stories rather than theories.

Rather than advance a theory or a promise of things to come, the phrase points the reader to the experience of "us" in the Program; it is our experience, not our theory. It is a subtle affirmation of the importance of stories rather than theories in our Program. We don't advance these promises and make this warranty as a matter of theory; it is a matter of fact and experience.

I love stories. When working with sponsees and newcomers, I try always to make a point with a story rather than a theory or an instruction.

Newcomers and sponsees love to argue with theories. But they cannot argue with stories. What will they say, "That is not what happened"?

Additionally, using stories to make a point allows the listener to identify with the story and integrate the lesson(s) completely.

In this clause, we are telling a newcomer, "These are the facts we are experiencing. If you identify with us, try it; you might like it. You have nothing to lose, and it might work for you. And we conditionally promise and warrant that, if you are like us, it will work for you." 🖋

Tricky Time Frame

We continue our deconstruction of the last clause of the Step Nine Contract.

As we saw in the last note, Bill describes the promises as a current, continuous, and experienced facts amongst us. The implied challenge issued to the reader is, "Are you so different? Try it; you might like it."

Then Bill adds a caveat—the timing of the promised fulfillment is temporally indeterminate: "They [these promissory experiences] are being fulfilled among us, sometimes quickly, sometimes slowly." The time frame could be long, or it could be short.

If a sponsee alleges breach of contract, asserting the promises are not coming true, we can reply with this statement of the facts as we are experiencing them. We can tell them, "Be patient, they still might come true for you. For us, it was sometimes slowly, sometimes quickly. Stick around for a while longer, extend the term, or better yet, renew the contract and do the Steps again."

The more challenging sponsees might argue further that the Step Nine Contract cannot be enforced; with no time frame, a judge would never be able to identify a breach of contract.

There is a good defense to this challenge: we have experienced progress, sometimes slowly and sometimes quickly, but there is always progress. If you are not experiencing progress, as we have done, then there might be a failure of consideration on your part, a failure to meet the standard of painstaking work. So, get to work, and work to the standard of performance required. That is the consideration for the Promises."

Is this ambiguous? I think so.

But it is constructive ambiguity.

Affirming the need for work

We continue our look at the last clause of the Step Nine Contract.

To refresh our memories, rather than make a promise, Bill states a fact: that the promises are coming true among us. It is a statement of our experience rather than our theories, followed by a temporal proviso, asserting that the results might come quickly or slowly, at least, that has been our experience.

Then Bill repeats the consideration required to enforce these promises of the Step Nine Contract.

"They will always materialize *if we work for them*." (Emphasis added.)

The concluding paragraph of this contract emphasizes the fact that the Program must be worked for the promises to be achieved. There is no free lunch; this is a contract and contracts include consideration.

The consideration is effort, and the initial clause of the Step Nine Contract stipulates the performance standard of effort; to wit—care and attention.

If there is a failure of consideration, the contract is not enforceable. You will not get the promises. You may be abstinent, but for serene sobriety, to enforce a claim to the benefits of these promises, you must do the work. ✒

A Painstaking Word Count

In the last note, I discussed the final clause of the Step Nine Contract and the consideration for the promises: work. I complete my review of the Step Nine Contract with a comment on the standard of performance required in connection with the "work."

The standard required is "painstaking." I have reviewed the dictionary meaning of painstaking, and I would like to continue with a word-counting exploration of the first 164 pages of The Big Book.

In the first 164 pages of our text, the word *painstaking* is only used once. But other words synonymous with painstaking are more frequent.

For example, words that align with painstaking, such as *persistence*, *continuous*, *effort*, *strenuous*, and *hard* are used eighty-four times. *Rigor*, portraying a stronger sense of painstaking, is used twice. The words *care* or *carefully*, which are included in the dictionary meaning of painstaking, occur forty times; twenty-five of these uses refer specifically to the standard that we impose on ourselves in our Program.

Highlighting the importance of effort in our Program, the word *work* is used eighty-seven times.

The emphasis on painstaking is affirmed when we look at its obverse, words which are the opposite of painstaking. *Careless*, the opposite of careful, is used twice, once in reference to our drinking and once in a warning to not be careless in our language. The word *easy* is used nine times, but it is not suggestive of an easy approach to the Program; seven of the nine uses of the word are phrases in opposition to any suggestion that it is easy to work the Program, phrases like, "it is not easy," or "it's easy to get off the beam" or "easy to let up." The word *casual* is used four times, but never in connection with our program; it is used in connection with our drinking, our pre-Program approach to spiritual life, and once to describe our AA meetings.

The promises of the Step Nine Contract are in consideration of working the Program to a painstaking standard. The consideration in the Contract is symmetrical and proportional. The benefits of the promises of the Step Nine Contract are non-trivial, and the required consideration is non-trivial. 🐟

PART TWO

The Lord's Prayer

Introduction

Every week, we close our ILAA Monday night online meeting by reading the Step Nine Promises and the Lord's Prayer.

After completing a week-by-week deconstruction of the clauses of the Step Nine Promises framed as a contract, I turned to the words and details of each clause of the Lord's Prayer: a focus that is often lost in quick recitation.

In writing these meditations on the Lord's Prayer, I am indebted to Emmet Fox, who, in an appendix to his *Sermon on the Mount*, shared his thoughts on the Lord's Prayer. That book, and his essays on this prayer in the appendix, were part of the AA Founders' canon, and are still worth reading.

Because we are lawyers, we pay attention to words. Lawyers are not alone in having a passionate regard for words. Literary scholars also pay close attention to words. They ponder the narratives, meaning and tone created by words. But as lawyers, we not only pay attention to the narrative, meaning and tone of words, we also focus on the consequences and implications that flow from the words.

In these notes, the meanings and consequences are discussed in the form of a legalistic exegesis, having regard to the tone, meaning and, more importantly, the consequences and implications of the words. ✒

The Prayer

> Our Father,
> Which art in Heaven,
> Hallowed be thy name.
> Thy kingdom come and thy will be done,
> On earth as it is in heaven.
> Give us this day our daily bread,
> And forgive us our trespasses, as we forgive those who trespass against us.
> Lead us not into temptation,
> Rather, deliver us from evil.
> For thine is the kingdom, the power and the glory,
> Forever and ever, amen."

Our Father

Many members of ILAA are citizens of the United States of America and many of them attend our regular ILAA Monday Zoom meeting. It is apropos, therefore, to start my discussion with a quote from that great American jurist, Oliver Wendell Holmes.

When asked for his views on religion, he replied, "My thoughts on religion are summed up in the first two words of the Lord's Prayer, 'Our Father.'"

What a wonderful summation. If those two words don't say it all, they say a great deal.

These words affirm we have a divine lineage. We start with an affirmation that God is our Father. As a father creates a child, so God has created us. As we are all made of the same substance as our earthly parents, we are made of the same substance of God.

And these words affirm the brotherhood of man. If God is the parent, we are His children, all of us. We are all related to a common Ancestor; we are all brothers and sisters. Because we are all children of God, between and among ourselves, no one can claim that any of us is greater than another. We all share the same root.

Lastly, these two words describe the character of God. God is a parent, a father. Good parents are kind, generous, and loving to their children. And we, who have been saved from a hopeless condition, know that God is good. He will care for us and guide us in the same way that a perfect natal parent would care for us and guide us. We, who experienced the benefits of Recovery, have understood Him thus.

Mr. Justice Holmes made an astute and pithy observation when he stated that his faith and spiritual life were summed up in the first two words of the Lord's Prayer. An observation with which I concur. 🌿

Which art in heaven

Lawyers study the structure and order of our legal system. In the common law tradition, we have Supreme Courts, Appeal Courts, Trial Courts and Chambers. There is a hierarchy. This clause is a statement of the structure and order of the universe. God is in heaven and man is on earth. There is a hierarchy.

God is on a different plane. He is in heaven and we are on earth. And because heaven is structurally above earth, God is above us.

All beings, both on earth and in heaven, have a role to play in the unfolding of the universe. God is in heaven, and I am on earth. God has His role, and I have mine.

This all points to a great, albeit implicit truth—God is not going to do my work, and I can't do His. ✒

Hallowed be Thy name

"Hallowed" means revered or consecrated.

"Be" carries the meaning of its object having a state, quality and nature. It is the present subjunctive case of that verb, expressing a state which is either wished or possible.

"Thy" is a direct reference to God. It is the genitive case of the noun thou, indicating possession. And "name" is the word by which a thing is known.

We will analyze this phrase, word by word, the first being "hallowed." To hallow is to revere, consecrate, worship, and obey.

Then we come to the verb *be*, which is in the present tense and subjunctive mood. It suggests that the referent of the adjective *hallowed* is not currently certain. In the subjunctive mood, the word carries the sense of a wish or expression of a possible state of God, as represented by His name. The indicative mood, "Hallowed *is* thy name," would have suggested certainty and an existing state of being. However, the translators use "Hallowed *be* thy name," invoking the subjunctive mood or, to use a legal term, the precatory sense, a possible and wished-for state. I hope his name is hallowed, and claim that to be true for me.

I submit that this construction and analysis are both beneficial for AAs and consistent with our AA understanding of a Higher Power.

We in AA trust and turn our lives over to God, as we have understood Him. We find a personal God, a God who is experienced by us, and known to us, through that experience. We find our own conception of God; we don't start with a theory or definition of God, we start with a small crack in the existential door and allow our experiences and "understoodings" to grow.

Rather than preconceived notions of God, we start with possibilities—possibilities which mature with and are informed by experience. We begin our relationship with God in the subjunctive rather than the indicative case. It is a precatory, hopeful and possible relationship based on past experience, not a certain, fixed relationship that is apart from our experience.

In this way, this clause of the Lord's Prayer squares perfectly with AA principles and sets the stage for the balance of the prayer.

And we pray that God be consecrated and revered. 🖋

Thy Kingdom Come

The next clause, "Thy kingdom come, Thy will be done, on earth as it is in heaven," is a precatory clause.

We live in hope and ask that God become our King and take charge. And as our King we hope that His will be done. And we hope that it will be done, if, as, and when it is in Heaven.

And all of this is to be done on earth and, necessarily, in our lives.

There is a feudal tinge to this with the reference to "King." Feudalism depended on the people offering themselves and their services to the king or the feudal lord in return for care and protection. In Step Three of our AA Program, this is mimicked when we offer ourselves to God, seeking His care and protection. Metaphorically, we are His subjects, and He is our King.

We ask that we be subject to God and His laws. We ask that His will be done on earth and in our lives. And we ask that this be done as if it were heaven.

This precatory clause in the Lord's Prayer is echoed in our AA Program. Let me elaborate with a fable vision.

I can see a feudal farmer just outside the king's domain, standing in his field, feeling alone and unprotected. The king is reputed to be just and kind. The farmer knows other farmers who have submitted to him, and they are happy and thriving. The farmer prays for the king to expand his domain to encompass and protect him, his family and his land, ensuring that he is safe and cared for. When it happens, he, too, is subject to the king.

As I farmed my life just outside of the AA kingdom, I saw others in the rooms of AA who were subject to God, the King of the Program. They seemed happy, joyous, and free. I asked God to enlarge His kingdom to encompass me, and I promised to strive to follow His will. I found my King. And He has been just and compassionate.

And every AA I know has found the same to be true. 🖋

Give us this day our daily bread

There are shades and layers of meaning in this clause.

First, let us consider bread as physical bread, the bread we eat. Bread is a common edible, and in this context, it serves as a metonym or proxy for all material sustenance necessary for human life, encompassing food and shelter.

Emmet Fox extends this view and posits that customers and other opportunities for income and wealth, with which we purchase sustenance and shelter, come to us from God. Accepting that proposition, when I serve my clients, I am serving God. When clients pay me, the wealth flows from God, through them, to me. Not a bad premise on which to tackle a day's work in the office—working for and paid by God.

Beyond this materialistic understanding, there is a spiritual perspective on bread as sustenance:

God provides us with metaphorical spiritual bread to nourish our souls. He supplies us with sustenance for our spiritual well-being.

These two dimensions of material and spiritual are enlarged with a temporal dimension; both dimensions of the bread are supplied daily.

This idea has several layers of meaning.

A material layer: it is dangerous to accumulate. When I accumulate material bread—wealth or property—I begin to think I am self-sufficient. From self-sufficient, it is a small and effortless step to self-centered and a belief that I can go it alone, without God. This is a risk of material success.

A spiritual layer of meaning: daily is continuous, a key term in our Program. I must seek fresh spiritual bread every day. The benefits of spiritual practice expire. Yesterday's spiritual bread will go stale; in fact, according to the Old Testament, if you eat yesterday's manna, you will be poisoned. If I believe that I don't have to receive my spiritual bread today; if I believe I am spiritually full or have had enough, I decline further portions. I become independent of God and full of myself. Spiritually prideful, ranking myself beside God, maybe there is not a power greater than myself. To be hungry every day, and desire fresh spiritual bread, is good.

I submit that three other dimensions are implicit in our quotidian request for bread.

First, every day we ask for bread and God asks in reply, "Will you let me feed you?"

If I answer, "Yes, please feed me," I am on the beam. I am ready and willing to ask for help. But when I am off the beam, I reply, "No thanks, not today. I don't need your food today; I have (accumulated) enough." Perhaps I think that I am doing Him a favor. More likely, my ego has pushed him aside; I am no longer hungry for His spiritual bread. I am separating myself from Him.

Another layer of meaning: eating is a personal experience. I cannot live on someone else's bread-eating; to get the benefit, I must eat my bread.

Finally, God needs us to actualize the bread. Bread uneaten is dormant; it does nothing. I must eat it, digest it, and convert it to energy. When I eat it, it becomes alive. It furthers His Kingdom

This simple clause has many layers of meaning that are truly wonderful. *

Forgive us our trespasses, as we forgive others

The adverb *as* is used when the author is comparing at least two things. Webster goes on to suggest that it is used to indicate, by comparison, the way that something happens or is done, and includes both the extent and degree. In this clause, the adverb modifies the verb *forgive*.

We are forgiven to the extent and degree we forgive. From our own lips, we set the terms, and by our own actions, we set the bar of forgiveness that will apply to us; I will be forgiven (only) to the extent and degree I have forgiven.

Every time I recite this prayer, I reaffirm this strict self-imposed rule.

If ever there was a time to be mindful of what I am saying, it is in reciting this prayer, particularly this clause.

You can rest assured I will consider these thoughts with greater care the next time I am racing through the Lord's Prayer at the end of a meeting. ✒

Lead us not into temptation, but deliver us from evil

This clause can be misunderstood to suggest that God might lead us into temptation; I do not believe this is correct.

God—as I have understood Him—will not tempt me and lead me astray.

There are two sub-clauses.

The first sub-clause is, "Lead us not into temptation."

If this clause were "Please don't lead me to temptation," it would be clearer and plainer.

But it does not say that. It frames us as passive followers, "lead us," with the possibility of temptation.

God leads me; at least, I have offered myself to be led as I practice Step Three. Will God lead me to temptation? I don't think so. But there are temptations in following God and striving to align my will with His will. The temptation is called *spiritual pride*. Thinking my striving has successfully aligned my will with God, I am inclined to demand that my wishes be followed; after all, they are from God.

I often joke, "God and I are so close it is sometimes hard to tell us apart," understanding that there is a dangerous kernel of truth in the joke.

And this temptation of spiritual pride is an *evil*, it is the evil that was identified by Milton in Paradise Lost, in the fall of Satan. It is the evil of every bleeding deacon in your Group's business meeting.

As my spiritual knowledge increased, I was more easily persuaded that I was right. I was spiritually advanced; therefore, I was right, and how could my authority be questioned? This subclause is a warning. A warning sounded by spiritual leaders through the millennia who warned their followers of the risks or temptations concomitant with spiritual growth.

I caution sponsees I work with, "Be very careful; spiritual knowledge amplifies your moral sense, for both good and bad."

We see the bad in AA; the sponsor that barks and commands, the AA brothers and sisters who insist that people see the Program their way, and the

AA service champions strutting and preening, while complaining bitterly about the lack of participants in AA service work.

These examples illustrate the spiritual risks associated with pride and temptation that can accompany spiritual growth.

There is an AA group in our town named Veritas. They have dealt with this temptation to pride with bit of sly humor. They refer to their Group, saying, "We are Veritas, first in humility since 1995."

I could copy this and introduce myself by saying, "My name is Andy, first in humility since 1977." Those who know me are likely to respond with loud guffaws. Those who don't know me will soon be chuckling, and laughter is a great tonic for spiritual pride.

The second sub-clause begins with the disjunctive preposition "but," which suggests that there is one path with more than one, at least two possible outcomes; if I follow this path, I will be tempted, but God can deliver me, or He will not. And the selection of the path is mine to make.

The prayer suggests that I must do something. In saying this prayer I am asking for help. And this I must do. God's help, in my experience, is not automatic. His default position is neutral; I must ask that I be delivered. If I don't, He will stand back and let the chips fall where they may. At least that is my experience.

The construction of this second sub-clause aligns with my experience. I have found His nature to be good, and He is interested in my happiness and contentment. He is a perfect Father. He is my creator. He loves me like a father, and He loves me as His creation. He would not "lead me to temptation," like some capricious deity looking for entertainment. But like a good father, he lets me learn. He will not do for me, what I should do for myself, unless I ask for help.

For me, these two sub-clauses are best constructed as: follow God, but understand that this can lead to spiritual pride, and remember to ask for His help in being delivered from this evil. ✒

For Thine is the kingdom, the power and the glory, for ever and ever, amen

I conclude with this note, which is closer to literary interpretation than legal construction.

A great Hollywood star said a great movie must have a solid opening and strong ending.

The opening clause, Our Father, is a statement of the nature and the brotherhood of man; it is a solid opening.

And this is a resounding end.

Next time you recite this prayer, think on this closing clause — feel the majesty and the rhythm of the words. ✿

PART THREE

Big Book Prayers

Introduction

After reviewing the Step Nine Contract and the Lord's Prayer clause by clause, I turned to Big Book prayers, closing each Monday night ILAA meeting with a short meditation on a Big Book prayer.

There are many prayers throughout The Big Book, and many stories telling of success in prayer. The Founders spent a lot of time praying or thinking about praying.

It has been said that all prayers fall into one of four categories:

1. Help!

2. Sorry!

3. Thanks!

4. Wow!

In this chapter I touch on 23 prayers from The Big Book, and I construe all but one of them to be Category 1 prayers—variations of help, please, guide me, show me, take away, etc. There is one prayer of thanks in Step Five.

It seems to me that this is apropos. The heart and foundation of our new spiritual life is desperation, a need for help. We need to be desperate enough to ask for help, we have to be "at the jumping-off place," life has to be too much for us.

We often say in the Rooms, "We are never given more than we can handle." Fortunately for me, I have found this to be untrue. Yet it is a useful untruth, and I am grateful for it. I often face more than I can handle, starting with alcohol, and every time, I am compelled to seek help from my Higher Power.

So it is appropriate that Help prayers are the most frequent prayers in AA.

Here are the selected 23 Big Book prayers.

The First Prayer

The first Big Book prayer is found on Page 13 of The Big Book.

> I humbly offered myself to God, as I then understood Him, to do with me as He would. I placed myself unreservedly under His care and direction. I admitted for the first time that of myself I was nothing: that without Him I was lost. I ruthlessly faced my sins and became willing to have my newfound Friend take them away, root and branch."

This brief prayer encapsulates Steps Three, Four, Five, Six and Seven of the Twelve-Step Program. In this prayer, Bill describes how he decided to turn his will and life over to God, faced his defects, admitted his shortcomings, became ready to have them removed, and asked God to remove them.

And the prayer that he used is strong; there are no half measures. Look at some of the phrases:

- "placed myself under God's care unreservedly" — without limit;

- "by myself I was nothing" — not just poor in spirit, but nothing;

- "without Him I was lost" — not just lacking power, but lost; and,

- "ruthlessly faced my sins" — not casually, but ruthlessly.

In this prayer, Bill used the familiar phrase "as I understood Him" for the first time, but with an additional word: "as I *then* understood Him." That small adverb *then* highlights Bill's experience of God up to that time. It was not a future faith but, rather, past knowledge and experience.

Bill does not suggest that he is counting on a past faith; nor does he suggest that he is looking for a future faith to come. Rather, he speaks of a present faith. And he does not claim a quality of faith, like deep faith or enduring faith: he claims only the faith he had at that time, "then."

As I consider this, *Faith* is probably not even the correct word for what he is talking about; he is describing his experience of God at that time, not a theological theory of faith or some future faith to come. For Bill, in this prayer, God is a simple, unvarnished, experiential fact.

Like Bill, we meet God where we are and how we stand. We meet God with our experience of God, up to that time, "God, as we *then* understood Him."

Bill understood God, at that time, to be a Friend. God had saved Bill from a hopeless condition. The Webster's Dictionary definition of *friend* includes descriptions like "a supporter who gives help," "someone on the same side," and "someone who is familiar and not an enemy." God, as Bill then understood Him, was all of the above.

So, this first prayer described in The Big Book contains a lot of the program that is to come. Four of the Twelve Steps, a strong word to match our hopeless disease, and a divine foundation on which to build a life—a hell of a first prayer. ❧

Offer and Acceptance

> God, I offer myself to Thee – to build with me and do with me as Thou Wilt. Relieve me of the bondage of self, that I may better do Thy Will. Take away my difficulties, that victory over them may bear witness to those I would help of Thy Power, Thy Love and Thy Way of Life. May I do Thy will Always!"

This prayer is from page 63 of The Big Book, the famous Step Three Prayer

The prayer is in four parts.

The first part is an offer: "I offer myself to Thee."

As lawyers, we know every contract is created in three parts: offer, acceptance and a communication of the acceptance.

When we offer this prayer, we assume that God will accept it. But how does He accept the it, and more interestingly, how does He, the offeree, communicate His acceptance to us, the offerors? For it is only after we know that He has accepted the offer that we have a binding contract.

There are, broadly speaking, two ways to communicate acceptance of an offer. The first is explicit; to communicate acceptance either verbally or in writing. The second is implicit; to communicate by "a course of conduct"; the offeree conducts himself "as if the contract were in place," thereby communicating acceptance.

When I made the offer in this prayer, God did not accept by speaking or writing, He communicated acceptance by "course of conduct." He began executing the contract, fulfilling the covenants made in the contract. He governed Himself as if the contract were in place.

This acceptance by course of conduct showed up as follows:

- the desire to drink was lifted;

- I was relieved from my self-centered and selfish attitudes and expectations that held me in bondage;

- many of my difficulties were removed (and stayed removed so long as I remembered that it was not for my sake, but so that others saw God in my life); and

- I received help in many areas of my life, including removing defects.

If you have done this Step, you have made an offer and have received knowledge of the acceptance by course of conduct.

But to receive knowledge of the acceptance, we must step out and act as if it were in place and allow God to respond.

At least that has been my experience.

Watch for acceptance of your offer by course of conduct; become aware of the positive changes in your life after committing to follow God's will and not your own. 🖋

The Dreaded Step Four

Step Four might be the most interesting part of The Big Book.

Before the prayer comes the Step. We have heard about the dreaded Step Four in meetings: our moral inventory.

It probably took some time to start. At every Step Four meeting, we hear how painful it will be. So we feared it, but we finally started it. And more importantly, finished it.

Now, turning to The Big Book, we find instructions for the Step Four prayer.

The instructions outline four conditions precedent to the Fourth Step prayer. First, we must complete an action, then affirm our agreement with two propositions, and lastly, a final instruction.

First an action: Upon completing our inventory, we are to review our Step Four carefully. We must study it carefully and digest it, reacquaint ourselves with the moral failings and harms we have listed.

We must reacquaint ourselves with just how bad we are.

Upon completing this careful review, we are to affirm two propositions, beginning with: "The first thing apparent (from this review) was that this world and its people were often quite wrong."

This is, I submit, surprising and counterintuitive.

I have just listed and carefully studied all my harms and moral defects. With this in mind, I should say something like, "The first thing apparent was how wrong I was and how bad I am, that I should be ashamed and apologize to the world."

If I had written the Big Book, it would say, "The first thing apparent was that I am a worthless bum."

Instead, Bill Wilson wrote, "The first thing apparent was that this world and its people were often quite wrong." Holy Mackerel.

This conclusion, which I am asked to affirm, is to my mind, both curious and counterintuitive.

Building on this counterintuitive thought, we are asked to affirm a second observation, consisting of two sub-clauses: "(1) To conclude that others were wrong was as far as most of us ever got" and

"(2) The usual outcome was that people continued to wrong us and we stayed sore." Unlike the first observation, when I stopped to think about many of the incidents in my inventory, this seemed to be a true and self-explanatory observation.

After agreeing with this observation, Bill gives us a final instruction. We are directed to replace an old habit with a new habit. We are to stop resenting the world, and instead treat them as if they were sick. Again, like the first, it was surprising and counterintuitive. After all, these were my enemies, people I had harmed. Again, Holy Mackerel.

One instruction, two affirmations and a fourth instruction. Now, Bill says we can say the Step Four prayer.

Paraphrasing, we are to ask God to help us show the people of the world, who were quite wrong, the tolerance, pity, and patience that we would give to a sick friend, then to pray to love them and not be angry with them. Finally, we conclude the prayer by saying, "Thy will be done."

The counterintuitive spirit continues in this prayer. Instead of praying about ourselves and our nasty, dreadful moral inventory, we pray about this world and its people, who were often quite wrong.

And we don't pray about them or for them, we ask for help for ourselves, to treat them differently.

That, my friends, is why I submit that the Step Four prayer is surprising and fascinating. ✒

The Ontological Questions

The next Big Book prayer is from page 68. We are still in the Step Four process.

> We ask God to remove our fear and direct our attention to what He would have us be."

As with the last prayer, there is a preamble with two conditions precedent to the prayer.

The first condition to be satisfied is another careful review of our Step Four inventory, focusing on fear. And we have another pen-to-paper exercise; we must write our deepest fears down on paper.

The second condition, an acknowledgment that fear is a corroding thread running through our lives.

Having completed these, we can turn to the prayer, which is not one, but two prayers, which are conjoined: "We ask God to remove our fear and direct our attention to what He would have us be."

The first prayer is a request that He remove our fear—not fears, plural; fear, singular. We are not asking for the removal of our casual fears of people, places, and things. We are asking God to remove our primal, our singular fear, the fear at the core of our beings. We ask for this primordial existential fear to be removed. This goes to the root of our being; it is ontological.

In the second prayer, we ask that He direct our thinking, pointing us to what He would have us be. Again, the prayer is ontological—what is our being, who we are? We don't ask for direction on what He would have us do, or say or how He would have us act; we ask that our attention be directed to what we should *be*.

Having done an inventory, we are now ready to tackle our existential fear and our ontological self.

And we do this with prayer. We cannot do it on our own, because this stuff is deep. ✎

Sex and More

The next prayer is also within the penumbra of Step Four.

Near the end of the discussion of the Step Four inventory process, Bill turns to sex, which occupies a lot of space in The Big Book.

Quoting from The Big Book:

> We asked God to mold our ideals (about sex) and help us live up to them."

When I first read this prayer, I thought, "Hang on here. Am I going to ask God to mold my ideas and ideals about sex? I am not sure God wants anything to do with my sex life. More importantly, I am not sure I want God even knowing about my sex life."

I delayed taking this drastic, prayerful step; I wanted the right moment to talk with my sponsor. At least that was the excuse I used for the delay.

Eventually, I broached the subject indirectly; I asked him, "Do you think God knows anything about sex?"

He rolled his eyes and said, "God probably knows a lot about sex. Adam might have discovered it, but God invented it. God might know something about it."

As the conversation evolved, I finally admitted that I was afraid to begin a conversation with my Higher Power about sex. I was convinced that God was vitally interested in my happiness and contentment. But, I asked, "Will that include my sexual satisfaction? At least the satisfaction I want?"

My sponsor's ocular muscles were getting a workout, rolling his eyes again. He said, "So this is all about your sexual satisfaction?"

I replied, "I can see you are going to try your usual trick and turn this into a defect. I don't see this as a defect; I see it as a long-held habit of thought, that does a small bit of damage."

But he had me when he asked, "Okay, were you serious about Step Three when you turned your will and life over to a Power greater than yourself? And were you serious about Step Two when you came to believe that a power greater than yourself could restore you to sanity?"

"And is your sex life sane and manageable, and do you have power over your sex drive?"

Clever sponsor, he had me back to Step One, admitting that I was powerless and unmanageable when it came to sex, and that my sex life was not entirely sane. Now I found myself rolling my eyes. As usual, he was right.

Starting the next day, on a blank sheet of paper, I wrote, "God, what should my ideal sex life look like?" Then, with pen to paper, I jotted down what came to mind, unloading a brain dump. And by God, with God, it worked. Gradually, over several weeks, my ideas about sex changed. My writing slowly transformed; my words and thoughts evolved on the paper over the next 14 days. What I wrote about sex on day one was very different from what I wrote on day fourteen. I don't know how; it was not conscious. But it worked. At the end, I was describing a better relationship with sex.

And my sponsees since then have used the same process and reported the same success.

Turn your mind to God, and just ask the question, pen to paper, "God, what should my ideal sex life look like?" And, as the Step Nine promise affirms, intuitively, you will know what to do.

But here is the real magic: In the years following, I have applied this tool to issues other than sex—work and my obsession with success, sports and my obsession with winning, life and my obsession with looking good.

It seems Bill used sex, which is dramatic, powerful, and familiar to us all, as a proxy for all my instincts. In all areas of life, with pen to paper, I have asked God to mold my ideas and help me live up to them. It works. It really does.[1]

---

1. The habit of prayerful automatic writing is good. You might want to check out Two Way Prayer. Father Bill W's website twowayprayer.org is a great source of information.

More Sex, and More

Next, we turn to two prayers, found on pages 69 and 70.

These prayers are still in the penumbra of the moral inventory, and we are also about sex. Either we have many problems in this area, or God has an inordinate interest in our sex lives.

In The Big Book, Bill instructs us to get ready for these two prayers, to assume the position, as it were. We are to think about every sex relation in our inventory; "we [are to] meditate on these [sex] incidents, episodes, or situations."

After we meditate, we ask God for four things:

- what to do about each specific matter,

- guidance in each situation,

- sanity, and

- the strength to do the right thing.

- Pause and meditate, then invoke the prayers.

> God, what do I do about (each specific matter)?
>
> And please give me guidance in these questionable situations, please give me sanity and the strength to do the right thing."

It is a great process for sex and other instincts and drives. It has worked for me and millions of others.

Bill discusses this process and prayer in the context of sex. But as discussed earlier, Bill seems to use sex as a proxy for all our instincts and drives. I have applied this prayerful process to sex, and it worked. I have also applied the same procedure to other instincts and drives like ambition, greed, fear, and others.

Try it. What do you have to lose?

Step Five Surprise

> God, I thank you from the bottom of my heart that I know you better."

This prayer (paraphrased) is from page 75 of the Big Book. If you are at this page, you have finished your Step Five and are preparing for Step Six. This prayer is to be said in the gap between these Steps.

Returning home, we find a place where we can be quiet for an hour, carefully reviewing what we have done. Quoting from the Big Book, "We thank God from the bottom of our heart that we know Him better."

In the Rooms we have many reasons to give thanks, but the reason we give prayerful thanks after Step Five and before Step Six is, as with so many of these prayers, unexpected and counterintuitive.

Let's review the work leading up to this prayer.

We have intensively investigated ourselves and our characters in Step Four. Then in our Step Five, we had a detailed discussion with another person about the exact nature of our wrongs. Completing Steps Four and Five, we have investigated and discussed ourselves and our innermost secrets; we have taken a deep dive into ourselves and our characters.

All this work was about me. As a result, I should know myself much better. I have identified defects, shortcomings, and instincts out of control. I have digested big parts of my character and my personality. I could give thanks that I know myself better.

Instead, we say the prayer noted above.

Do we thank God that we know ourselves better? No, we thank God that we know *Him* better.

It doesn't seem right, but it is the truth. It was my experience, and it is an experience shared by millions of AAs. Coming to know myself was the action, but the consequence was coming to know my Higher Power.

It echoes Bill's earlier statements about Steps Four and Five.

To paraphrase Bill's description of the whole process: After piercing our pride and illuminating every twist to character, every dark cranny of the past, we are delighted. We begin to feel the nearness of our Creator; we have a spiritual experience. We are on the Broad Highway, walking hand in hand with the Spirit of the universe.

This prayer reflects and confirms the counterintuitive consequence of Step Five; we know ourselves better, but what do we thank God for? Surprise! We give thanks that we know Him better. 🖋

The Last Item Before Takeoff

We are still on page 75, getting ready to transition from Step Five to Step Six.

From The Big Book, "We returned home, found a place where we could be quiet for an hour, and carefully reviewed what we have done. We thanked God from the bottom of our heart that we know Him better."

Then we have this short prayer:

> We asked God if we had omitted anything."

I think of a pilot sitting at the end of the runway, engines spooling up. He reviews his takeoff checklist; the tanks are full, the flaps are down and his seat belt is tight.

We are sitting on the Step Six runway. There is a checklist, like a checklist a pilot reviews before taking off in his airplane. We are confident we are working with a Higher Power that could restore us to sanity. Check. We have turned our will and lives to a God that we have understood. Check. We conducted a thorough inventory, then talked to ourselves, God and another human being. Check and check and check.

Back to our pilot, he pauses before pushing the throttles forward and asks, "Have I forgotten anything?" One last quick review, then he pushes the throttles forward and the wings gain lift from the air.

This is the last item on our Program checklist. Before we roll down the Step Six runway, we ask God if we have omitted anything. After this final check, we can take off to Step Six.

We have done a lot of preparatory work, and we are on the spiritual tarmac, ready to start Step Six. We review all that we have done to this point. Then we stop, pause and say this prayer, "Is there anything we have forgotten?"

In the momentary quiet, other things can come to mind before we push the spiritual throttle forward. When these are done, then we are ready to move down the spiritual runway and get God's air under our wings.

I have had sponsees push back. They assert they have not missed anything; they don't need to ask God.

I often tell them, "If you don't want to ask God if you have omitted anything, we can ask your wife. We can ask her if you have omitted anything. But you might find it safer to ask God."

"Have I omitted anything?" The last check before we start down the spiritual runway. ✑

Willing, Two Dimensions

Now we move to page 76 of The Big Book.

In the last prayer, we asked God if we had omitted anything in our Program process. Assuming we waited for the answer and it was negative, we have completed this phase of the Program.

We have a sense of the exact nature of our defects. Now we turn to the task of ridding ourselves of these defects. This is a two-step process, Steps Six and Seven.

The first of the two steps, Step Six, requires that we reach a mental state. We must be able to say to ourselves that we are entirely willing to have God remove all these defects of character.

Not everyone reaches this state of willingness. Anticipating this, Bill slides an optional prayer before the Step Six:

> If we still cling to something we will not let go, we ask God to help us be willing."

This sentence seems to be optional. It says that it is only required if I have identified a defect and declare that I will not let it go.

An honest declaration is something God can work with when we ask for willingness. But I don't usually make an honest declaration.

Often, when I say that I am willing, I deceive myself. I have confidently said, "I am willing to have all my defects removed," but find myself continuing to enthusiastically practice the defects I am willing to have removed. Excessive fear, anger, and judging others: these are all defects I declared I was willing to have removed, but I continue to practice them. My actions speak louder than my intentions.

My capacity to lie about my willingness is astounding. I can genuinely feel and believe I am willing, but the defects persist. The facts cannot lie. Whatever I think or believe, the willingness is not there.

Eventually, I see the self-deception and say the prayer, "God help me be willing." But there is often a long period of suffering and difficulties as I continue to practice my defects. All the while declaring my willingness to have them removed.

After many experiences of lengthy and painful self-deception, I learned to assume I will have some degree of mendacity when I vouch for my willingness. Rather than wait to prove my dishonesty with a mismatch of stated willingness measured against actions, I have adopted a standard operating procedure. I ask God to help me be willing, all the time and every time I approach these Steps. Which, at a minimum, is annually, after my yearly Personal Inventory.

So, for me, this is not an optional prayer; it is part of my standard Step procedure.

It saves time, energy, and embarrassment. ✎

The Step Seven Prayer - A Paraphrase

The oft-repeated Step Seven prayer is found on page 76.

It reads:

> My Creator, I am now willing that You should have all of me, good and bad. I pray that You now remove from me every single defect of character which stands in the way of my usefulness to You and my fellows. Grant me strength as I go out from here to do Your bidding. Amen."

This prayer is uncomplicated but complex. It is so big and there is so much meat, I don't know where to start. Therefore, I am not prepared to expound upon this prayer.

Instead, I will paraphrase and, in so doing, highlight features of the prayer that I have experienced.

My Creator, God, the Universal Force and Flow, I have experienced you and have understood You to be involved in my life.

I know that You will not fix everything around me. You will not change my circumstances. You will only work within me, and in so doing, You will change my life and me.

At this moment, I want You to have all of me, both good and bad,

I ask that You possess me completely, the entirety of my being.

I ask for Your help, for I can do no more, and I need You enough to ask for this.

This desire to abandon myself to You is true in this instant and authentic in this prayer, but I know it will pass. All I can say is, I want You to have all of me, good through bad; me, as I am right now.

I have some defects of character.

You and I have talked about them.

I hope I am willing to have them removed, but I know from past experience that I am probably not as willing as I think.

Please overcome any latent reservations I have but don't see.

Please either remove them from me or show me what You would have me do to have them removed.

I know that You will only deal with one defect at a time, and it will be a defect that You need to be removed, not one that I think should be removed.

That is how I have understood You to operate.

You have not been wrong yet, and I trust in your judgment.

In conclusion: At this moment, I desire that You have all of me, possess me, and that I flow with You.

I am going to get back to work now, and I am going to try to remember to do Your bidding and follow Your instructions.

Please give me strength, as I go about Your business.

God, so I know we have ended this moment together, I say, amen." ✏

The Specific and the General

The preceding prayer was the Step Seven prayer. I paraphrased it to show my experience of the prayer. We have requested that our defects be removed. That may take some time. Even though we may still have them, it is time to move to Step Eight.

In Step Eight, we are now going to make amends. We are directed "to go out to our fellows and repair the damage done in the past." We are to attempt to "sweep away the debris which has accumulated out of our effort to live on self-will and run the show ourselves."

Now we turn to Page 76—the only Step Eight prayer in The Big Book:

> If we haven't the will to do this, we ask until it comes."

For me, this is another optional prayer, but it is better viewed as required.

At first, it seems optional—I only need to say it if I don't have the will. But, as with the earlier optional prayers, to save time and misery, I have learned the better course is to always say it.

Optional or not, I misunderstood it for years. I thought it was a prayer for willingness to make amends to the people I had listed in my Step Eight. But I have come to see the scope of the prayer is greater than my Step Eight list; it is a prayer to make amends to the whole world. That includes all the defects identified in my earlier lists, as well as many more.

The prayer reads, "If we haven't the will to do this." Turning to The Big Book, we see that the determiner *this* references the two immediately preceding sentences.

The first sentence is, "Now we go out to our fellows and repair the damage done in the past." And the second sentence affirms this broader frame: "We attempt to sweep away the debris which has accumulated out of our effort to live on self-will and run the show ourselves."

There are no words of limitation in these sentences. The first sentence does not stipulate "some of the damage," or "the damage that we have listed," it references all "the damage done in the past." And the second sentence does not limit the sweeping of debris to the debris arising from the harms listed in Step Eight; it is everything that has accumulated out of our efforts to run the show.

This is a prayer to be willing to repair all the damage and sweep up all the debris accumulated in my self-willed life.

With a task this large, it is no surprise that this optional prayer should become a standard operating procedure in the amends processes. 🖋

Risky Business

There is only one Step Eight prayer, but there are four Step Nine prayers. I will consider them one at a time. Turning to Page 79, we find the first Step Nine prayer.

First, as we make our amends:

> We ask (our Higher Power) that we be given strength and direction to do the right thing, no matter what the personal consequences might be."

Some Big Book Step prayers change the meaning of the Step. For example, in the Step Seven prayer, we are to ask for God to remove every "single defect of character," while Step Seven refers to "all these shortcomings." The prayer departs from the step in individualizing each defect. And the determiner *these* in Step Seven, points to the defects identified in our Step process, a limitation not found in the

Step Seven prayer; we ask that every defect, identified or not, be removed.

However, this Step Nine prayer fits perfectly with the Step Nine instructions. Step Nine stipulates that we are to do anything required, with a proviso: We cannot do anything that might harm the amendee or others. This prayer does not depart from the Step Nine instructions. It has no words of limitation and is restricted only to a request for strength and direction "to do the right thing."

And this prayer highlights the risks that may be involved. We are told to have no regard for our personal safety. Even if our personal safety might be compromised, we are to disregard our normal impulses, and do whatever it takes.

I often hear AAs say that in Step Nine we leave the outcomes to God. When I hear this said I wonder if the speaker is not also hoping that God will minimize the potential risks to his personal safety. But that is not the language of the prayer. We are to ask for help "no matter what the personal consequences might be." I think that a fair reading of the prayer suggests "personal" refers to the amendor, rather than the amendee.

Often consequences of amends are not pleasant, and one could be forgiven if an amend triggers bad consequences for the amendor, and he says in response, "This is all wrong. I am doing the right thing; I should be praised, but this hurts." When these unpleasant or dangerous consequences occur, or look likely to occur, the prayer is for the strength to deal with them. It is not a request to evade them or a prayer for different outcomes. What will be will be, and I should only ask God to give me the strength to deal with it.

This prayer also asks for direction from our Higher Power; this might be God, Allah, or just the unfolding flow of the universe. Regardless, we need direction. At this point, it would be prudent to remember that our undirected thinking and actions resulted in the amends having to be made. We would be wise to pick a different way of developing our thoughts and actions in making the amend. ✤

Drastic Stuff

The next prayer is suggested in the context of any drastic amend. Some amends are minor, but some are major, drastic.

In case I have a drastic amend coming up, there is a short but critical checklist of things to be done before making the amend, and the last item on the checklist is a prayer.

Here is the four-part checklist:

Before taking drastic action, which might implicate other people,

1. we secure their consent, and if we have

2. obtained permission, we then

3. consult with others, and finally we say the prayer,

4. we ask God to help,

Many of the consequences of our actions, the harms and damages we have caused, were complex and non-trivial. Our amends must be symmetrical and proportional to the harms done. Some of the harms we did had a wide impact; therefore, the consequences of our amends are sometimes drastic and can have a wide impact. And this prayer focuses on the amends that might involve other people.

Drastic describes something likely to have a substantial or far-reaching effect. An amend can meet this definition. These are the amends for which we need this checklist and prayer for help.

If we have a drastic amend which involves other people, we follow the checklist, a series of questions: Will it affect others? Have we communicated with them? Have we obtained their consent—not our sponsor's consent, but the consent of the affected people? Have we consulted with others, and have they concurred with our proposed action? And the last item on the checklist is the prayer, "We ask God to help."

Once these checklist items are complete, we must not shrink.

Making drastic amends without completing the checklist and the prayer taught me the value of the checklist and the prayer. I often had to make amends for the amends.

I have learned to complete the whole checklist, including the last item, the prayer. The most important item on the list.

It is not a prayer asking God to fix things. It is a repetition of the prayer for help and strength. Help in making the amend and the strength to make the drastic amend regardless of the personal consequences.

In summary, before a drastic amend, recognize, consider, seek required consents, discuss with trusted advisors, then pray for help.

The whole checklist should be completed. Otherwise, you might be like the pilot who tried to land his plane without lowering the wheels. It was the last item on his checklist.

Ignoring the last item and forgetting to lower the landing gear, the landing was hard, with lots of sparks and noise. If I forget the prayer, the results of a drastic amend can be similarly sub-optimal and exciting. ⚓

Screwing Around?

On page 82 of The Big Book, Bill Wilson instructs us to pray in the context of making amends for any extramarital affairs.

The prayer instruction is simple:

> Pray about it (both the harm and the amend), having the other one's happiness uppermost in mind."

The context of this prayer is marital infidelity. The context is powerful and dramatic. The reference to philandering gets our attention. But I wonder if marital infidelity might be a proxy for all breaches of trust or violations of good faith in all our relationships.

I have not had to make amends for marital infidelity. But I have betrayed trust and broken faith in other ways. My life has included infidelities large and small, both advertent and inadvertent. Business and the practice of law have provided me with ample opportunities for betrayals. In sports I have broken faith with teammates, opponents and referees by lacking grace and displaying anger: infidelity. In social situations, I have gossiped: infidelity. In business I have broken promises: infidelity.

I have learned this prayerful instruction can apply in all examples of breach, betrayal, and infidelity; it works in any relationship where normative or appropriate expectations have been dishonored or breached.

Failure to give a full effort on behalf of a client, rude behavior on the sports field, telling secrets, gossiping or subtle stealing of time; these and other harms and damages can be treated with the same prayer: Turn my mind to God and dwell exclusively on the other's happiness.

Following this prayerful instruction is spiritually sound, and practically, it is good. After saying this prayer, I will rise from my knees with the right attitude towards the person with whom I must make an amend, dramatically increasing the chances of a good outcome. ♦

Patience, Kindliness, Tolerance and Love – PKTL

This is the last Step Nine prayer.

Bill directs us to:

> ...clean house with the family, asking each morning in meditation, that our Creator show us the way of patience, tolerance, kindliness and love."

Cleaning house with the family, we change our behaviors. We stop kicking the dog and yelling at the children.

This is a good start, but more is demanded of us; we must demonstrate Patience, Kindness, Tolerance and Love. We alcoholics, newly sober, don't have much practice in this new way of family life. We need help, and with this prayer we ask God to show us the way. And we list four tools that God uses: Patience, Kindliness, Tolerance and Love.

It seems to me that Bill uses "cleaning house with the family" in the same way he used extramarital philandering, in the previous prayer, as a proxy for other close relationships.

The tools to amend family relations can apply to other relationships, especially proximate relationships.

Practicing law, we have many proximate relationships. We are close with clients, partners, and staff; with other lawyers, judges, and regulators; we have many communities of close relationships. We can stop barking at staff or abusing other lawyers. That is a good start, but we need more.

We clean house at home by demonstrating Patience, Kindliness, Tolerance and Love. We can clean house in other relationships, with partners, clients, staff and other lawyers or judges with the same formula. We are to practice these principles, Patience, Kindliness, Tolerance, and Love, in all our affairs and all our close relationships.

Initialisms are a mnemonic, the initialism for the four tools is PKTL. A sponsee taught me this initialism years ago. I still use it.

When I am on the spiritual beam, in the morning I ask God to show me the way of PKTL at home and in the office. As the morning prayer wears off through the day, I use the abbreviation PKTL as a reminder. PKTL: Patience, Kindliness, Tolerance, and Love.

PKTL, is a supplement to our grandmothers' admonition to "count to 10." 🖋

A Habit of Inquiry

We move now from making amends, in Step Eight and Nine, to Step Ten personal inventories.

The next prayer, from page 84, is associated with Step Ten spot check inventories:

We continue to watch for selfishness, dishonesty, resentment and fear, and, when they crop up, we offer a simple prayer:

> We ask God at once to remove them (selfishness, dishonesty, resentment and fear)."

Asking God, as I have understood Him, to remove selfishness, dishonesty, resentment, or fear is a great idea. But how should we expect to receive an answer? Should we expect a hallucinatory white light experience, words written by a heavenly finger on the wall or a deep booming voice from above?

In my experience, the corrective process starts with self-examination, "watch(ing) for selfishness, dishonesty, resentment and fear." This simple act of observation turns my mind and attention to the problem, and turning my mind to the problem triggers change; my subconscious mental faculties start to work on moving my soul to the opposite of selfishness, dishonesty, resentment, or fear. It is as if I am saying to myself, "Andy, you are being selfish, dishonest, resentful, or fearful," and articulation of the problem begins the healing process.

Having focused my mind on the problem, asking God for help furthers the healing process. Turning my mind to God elevates my soul and changes my vantage point as I look upon the world and see there is an unfolding of the universe. My perceptions change with the change in vantage point, and my attitudes change from "The universe is out to get me" to "God is in charge." These changes trigger favorable mental consequences.

I conclude this note with two observations.

First, the prayer instruction starts with a personal inventory. This habit of inquiry is a great habit. It is not omphaloskeptic—unfocused, self-absorbed navel-gazing; it is disciplined self-awareness, with specific questions: Am I being selfish, dishonest with myself, full of resentments, or does fear govern me?

The inquiry opens the healing door, which, as argued above, begins to have immediate unconscious effect. This habit of inquiry is a great start, made better when followed with the habit of prayer.

Second, the prayer is punctuation-free. "We ask God at once to remove them [the selfishness, dishonesty, resentment, or fear]." The phrase "at once" is not marked with any punctuation to indicate whether it is modifying "we ask God" or "to remove them." Perhaps it modifies both. We ask God for help at once, and ask that they be removed at once. Asking God at once squares with Step Ten, and the salutary effects of asking the question and turning to God are immediate: at once.

The absence of punctuation would seem to be intentional. ♪

A Quotidian Prayer

We inventory ourselves continuously, and regularly. Some AAs do inventories annually, quarterly, and monthly. Almost all successful AAs do them daily, and this prayer from Page 85 focuses on the daily inventory.

The preamble for this prayer highlights its quotidian nature: "Every day is a day when we must carry the vision of God's will into all our activities." The preamble is followed by this prayer:

> God, how can I best serve Thee – Thy will, not mine, be done."

It may seem trite and unnecessary to say, "thy will, not mine, be done." But I submit that there is merit in this reminder.

In the AA Rooms, we often hear expressions like, "I need to do the next right thing," or "I want to be my better self."

These are good thoughts. But in these well-intentioned and heartfelt statements, there are a lot of *I's* and *me's*. They remind me of the other common expressions we hear: I can do this; I can do the next right thing; I can be a better me; I can do better.

Again, many *I's* and *me's*.

This prayer points our minds and hearts away from *me* and *I*, toward something higher.

Instead of *me* deciding what I think is the next right thing, *me* thinking about how I can be a better me, or *me* thinking about how I can do better, this prayer turns my mind toward my Higher Power.

And the interrogatory "How can I best serve Thee?" opens my ears to hear either what He is telling me to do next or how He is telling me to be better.

This prayer is a great reminder, a great addition to a morning meditation and evening quiet time. And it will not wear out with use. Feel free to use it every day and throughout the day.

"God, how can I best serve Thee – Thy will, not mine, be done."

Beyond Quotidian

The last prayer we looked at was our Step Ten quotidian prayer.

> God, how can I best serve Thee? Thy will, not mine, be done."

It is an excellent daily prayer, and it is important to emphasize that it will not wear out with use; feel free to apply it when doing other personal inventories. It can be used with your weekly, monthly, and annual inventories.

Whenever and however you do an inventory, throw this prayer at the wall. It will stick every time.

The Missing Element

The following prayer, from page 86 of The Big Book, focuses on our nightly review.

Every night, we review our day, and there is a checklist of questions for the end of the day. It can be used like an airplane pilot's landing checklist.

Drawing on The Big Book questions, I developed an evening and a morning checklist. They can be found on the Home Page of the4thdimension.ca under "Worksheets." Click on the menu and click on "Checklists." And you can order hard copies, plasticized to allow you to use an erasable marker to check the items when completed.

The evening checklist is like a pilot's checklist for landing. The questions point to common problems, like selfish thinking, worry, remorse, dishonesty and gossip. We are not unique in having these problems; everyone has them, but we AAs are particularly sensitive. We must deal with them quickly or they cause problems.

When our evening or landing checklist is complete, we are to recite an evening prayer:

> We ask God's forgiveness and inquire what corrective measures should be taken."

Two things: First, we ask His forgiveness and second, we ask what we can do to make it right.

The request for forgiveness is one of the four principal prayer types: Sorry, thanks, help and wow. This is 'sorry.'

Then we ask, "What corrective measures should be taken?" We don't ask God to make it right. That is our job. We don't delegate the corrective actions to Him, we ask Him for knowledge of His will for us and, in particular, His instructions to right any wrongs of the day.

But there is a crucial element missing in The Big Book instructions around this prayer.

Fortunately, an early sponsor set me on the right track. Together we had reviewed Step Ten, and when we came to this part of the instruction, he added an important element to the instruction. He said, "In the evening, after you ask what corrective measures should be taken, don't just go to bed; you have to stop and listen!"

Without missing a beat, he continued, "If you pause for even a moment, God might get a word in edgewise. But you have to pause, and you have to listen."

What a difference it makes to stop and listen after asking God a question. 🌱

Grammar Is Important

Step Eleven directs us to seek to improve our conscious contact with God, using both prayer and meditation. In the Step Eleven prayer:

> We ask God to direct our thinking, especially asking that it be divorced from self-pity, dishonest or self-seeking motives."

I memorized this prayer and used it for years.

I thought I was saying it correctly. But I was mistaken. Working with a sponsee one day, I read him this prayer and realized I had misremembered the wording. I would ask that God keep me from "self-pity, dishonesty or self-seeking." I unconsciously dropped the word "motives."

But the prayer is precise. I am to ask for help with self-pity and, separately, for help with dishonest or self-seeking motives. *Dishonest* and *self-seeking* are adjectives modifying the noun *motives*. *Self-pity* is a noun with no descriptive adjectives. If Bill had intended *self-pity* to describe the word *motive*, he would have made it an adjective, using the gerund, *self-pitying*.

The sentence has three elements: self-pity as a behavior or attitude, dishonest motives and self-seeking motives.

Misremembering the prayer, I had been asking God to keep me from self-pitying, dishonest, and self-seeking behaviors or attitudes. When I saw the whole prayer and noticed that the word *motives* referred to those classified as *dishonest* and *self-seeking*, I amended my prayer. I asked God to help with my self-pity and then help with my dishonest and self-seeking motives. I noticed a change.

A motive is like a train engine with a series of freight cars. These cars are the behaviors that follow the motives, the behavioral cars. The train engine pulled self-seeking tank cars of temper, boxcars of gossip, and flatbed cars of cutting corners. The dishonest locomotive pulled passenger cars of justified anger, covered wagons of envy, and a caboose of pride.

Remembering the word *motives*, I was asking God to help with all the train cars being pulled by the engines of dishonesty and self-seeking.

Noting all the words and paying attention to the grammar, the effect of the prayer was more powerful and comprehensive. ✒

A Compelling Case

We are still on page 86, but now the evening has come and gone. It is morning and, following The Big Book directions, we are reviewing our day ahead.

We may see something difficult in our calendar or task list. It could be a contentious meeting, a difficult phone call, an important decision, or an anxious something. If we see anything contentious or problematic, we pause, and "ask God for inspiration, an intuitive thought or decision."

Bill received his spiritual habits and knowledge from the Oxford Group. Bill probably learned of inspiration and intuitive thought from an Oxford Group practice called Guidance. Oxford Groupers practicing Guidance would begin with a spiritual reading, then sit quietly and ask God for specific instructions for the day ahead. After asking God for this guidance, they stopped and listened. Sitting with a pad and pencil, they would write down thoughts and ideas that came to mind—inspirations, intuitive thoughts, and decisions. The Oxford Grouper would be God's amanuensis.

In the prayer we ask for an inspiration, an intuitive thought, or a decision. We don't get a booming voice from the clouds or a finger writing instructions on the wall. For me, it is a still, small voice of intuition. And I have to listen quietly.

However, in my experience, there is another way God communicates. He creates a compelling case to indicate a direction or action. When I lift the problem to Him, asking for help, and I don't get an intuitive thought, I wait and watch. Circumstances begin to develop such that it becomes perfectly natural to go in a direction; after watching and waiting, I can see a compelling case for a decision or a course of action.

Doors open and doors close. If I am mindful, I can see that I am being guided along a path. The compelling case might be a comment, an opportunity, or a disappointment. It might be a fresh development, challenge, or some other indicator of the "decision" to be made.

So, I pray for inspiration and receive an intuitive thought or a compelling case. But in either case, I check the answer with my sponsor. 🌿

Pure Motives Hide My Ego

We turn now to the third of five Step Eleven prayers in The Big Book, a prayer we use to conclude our morning meditation.

It is longer than many of the other prayers:

> We usually conclude the period of meditation with a prayer that we be shown all through the day what our next step is to be, that we be given whatever we need to take care of problems. We especially ask for freedom from self-will and are careful to make no request for ourselves only. We may ask for ourselves, however, if others will be helped. We are careful never to pray for our own selfish ends."

The prayer is in two parts.

In this note, I will look at the first part, which is, "We ask to be shown what our next step is to be."

For years I said this prayer in the morning.

During the day, I would say to myself, "Do the next right thing." It was a good sentiment and a good habit of thought. Practicing this meant that I was living in each moment, living in the present and focusing only on the next right thing. And who could argue with doing the right thing?

But over the years, I realized that I was not paying attention to my language: When I said, "I want to do the next right thing," there was an unspoken proviso which gained strength through the day, "*I* will determine the next right thing." As the day progressed, I lost track of God. I lost the habit of asking God for direction on the next right thing.

Not only was I unconscious of this loss of habit, my motives hid the problem from sight. I felt justified and pure because my motives were pure: I wanted to do the next right thing. And those pure motives hid the unconscious self-centered agenda; I wanted to do *my* next right thing.

I became more careful with my language because it is all about me and my judgment if I forget to include God.

It is better when I say, "I want to do the thing that God needs done," or, "Thy will be done."

It reminds me that God is in charge. ✐

Words Fail, Spirit Succeeds

In the preceding note, I considered the first part of this prayer. This is the second part of the prayer, which concludes our morning meditation.

In the second part, we ask "that we be given whatever we need to take care of problems."

This is followed by a series of qualifications and provisos defining and limiting this request: "We especially ask for freedom from self-will, and are careful to make no request for ourselves only. We may ask for ourselves, however, if others will be helped. We are careful never to pray for our own selfish ends."

It is complicated.

But at its heart, the prayer is simple. We ask for whatever we need to take care of problems. And there are no boundaries.

However, Bill seems to say, "Just a minute, we need *some* boundaries. In asking for whatever we need, we might start asking for the wrong things. Therefore we should also ask for freedom from self-will."

So, ask for whatever you need, but especially ask for freedom from self-will.

Then, Bill seems to say, "There is too much wiggle room with that proviso. The prayer for whatever we need should contain no request for ourselves only."

We ask for whatever we need, but first, to be released from self-will and, to emphasize the point, never ask for anything for ourselves only.

Then to complicate things, Bill's language suggests, "Let's not go too far. There is an exception to the limiting proviso. We can ask for something for ourselves if it will help others."

Finally, Bill throws his hands up in the air and concludes, "What I mean is, we should never pray for our own selfish ends."

Through all the back and forth, we can see the spirit of the prayer; throughout the day, we must ask for help and do God's will, but watch out! Self-seeking motives can sneak in the back door. ✒

An Important Habit

We have now completed our daily preparation and concluded our meditation. Time to get in the game, time to start the day and there is a prayer for the day.

We are instructed to ask God throughout the day for the right thought or action, and to pray, over and over:

> Thy will be done."

This prayer is to be habitual, and habits have triggers. The trigger for this habit is agitation or doubt. Whenever we feel agitated or doubtful, repeat the prayer.

But it is hard to pull the trigger on a prayer habit when things are going badly. To focus on draining the swamp when alligators are snapping requires a discipline that most of us lack. I need to have this prayer ready and at hand.

For me it is important to practice this habit, at all times of agitation, large and especially small, so it is habituated and ready. I have found it helpful to habituate this prayer with small agitations, the easy ones. Then, when the big ones hit, as they will, I am practiced and habituated.

As a mnemonic, I keep the initialism PPL in my mind: Pause, Pray and Listen. A handy mnemonic; in moments of doubt or agitation, PPL.

It is difficult at first, and feels unnatural, but Bill assures us, and I second the assurance, that "After we have tried this for a while, what used to be the hunch or occasional inspiration gradually becomes a working part of the mind."

We Are Specialists

Our final prayer is:

> Ask Him in your morning meditation what you can do each day for the man who is still sick."

It is on page 164, the final page of the text portion of The Big Book.

I would make several observations.

First, it is quotidian. The answers to this prayer are like Old Testament manna provided to the Israelites in the desert. I cannot store it even for a day; it will not last. It must be refreshed daily.

Second, as the Nike expression goes, "Just do it." If I think I can forego this morning prayer, I am lazy, self-confident and foolish all at the same time.

Just do it, and do it in the morning. Set my day up.

Third, I am to ask God to show how I can be of service to the man who is still sick. And though this prayer may include all persons we deal with, I believe the context of the prayer points my heart and mind to my fellow alcoholics as the sick persons I should serve.

For me, this implies a caution. Don't try to fix the world. My primary task is working with alcoholics; don't worry about the rest.

And finally, an enormous proviso follows this prayer: "The answers will come if your own house is in order."

If the answers are not coming, my own house may not be in order. I can take some time and put it in order. And I note, the prayer does not say, "If no answers come, wing it." If the answers don't come, it is okay if I remain silent and wait for further instructions.

But it is always better if, while I am silent, I am working the Steps and seeking another spiritual awakening.

We hope you enjoyed *Sober Covenants*.
If you are looking for more content to
Grow, Empower, and Motivate Spiritual
growth, visit Andy C. at
the4thdimension.ca

For more books, blog posts, podcasts,
printable worksheets,
and to subscribe to his weekly newsletter.

www.ingramcontent.com/pod-product-compliance
Lightning Source LLC
Chambersburg PA
CBHW070313010526
44107CB00004B/323